Revised edition

Put your Rear into Gear

Understanding and breaking free from Procrastination

by Jeanine Reiss

Lifeworks Publishing Ltd.
Kelowna   British Columbia   Canada

Published by
LIFEWORKS PUBLISHING LTD
372 Christleton Avenue
Kelowna, BC V1Y 5H7
Tel/fax: (250) 868-2054
Toll free: 1-866-868-2054
Website: WWW.lifeworkspublishing.com

National Library of Canada Cataloguing in Publication Data

Reiss, Jeanine, 1962-
  Put your rear into gear

  Includes index.
  ISBN 0-9730095-1-9

  1. Procrastination. I. Title.
BF637.P76R43 2002   155.2'32   C2002-910399-1

Printed and bound in Canada by Hignell Printing Ltd.

I dedicate this book to
my mom and dad who,
each in their own way,
encouraged me to be curious.

Table of Contents

Introduction

Dilly-dalling, lally-gagging, horsing around…
Whether it was to avoid having to eat our pureed carrots, pick up our toys, or steer clear of our auntie's kisses, most of us became masters at procrastination even before we set foot in preschool. Fortunately, at that age delay didn't matter too much. The implications were usually short lived and the dragging of our tender heels could in most cases be easily explained: we considered the task or chore to be yucky, or no fun.

While our young and not yet fully developed minds may have considered these reasons to have considerable clout, with maturity comes the ability to reach beyond the scope of what is pleasurable for what is right, better, more important, or downright necessary.

With the realization that life is not all fun and games, and the added bonus that as adults we no longer have to obey our parents, but instead can more or less pursue our own needs and wants, it would seem our lingering days were over:
We are free! Free at last, to get up and go, to sail around the world, to pursue that career, to get into shape, to make new friends, to fix that leaky roof, to do the dishes, to.…

 And often we will do just that. We make changes, however big or small, to better our circumstances or to make life more invigorating and meaningful.

Then there are the times that, no matter how dire the need or how burning the want, we just can't seem to get going.…

Part I

Understanding
Procrastination:

·1·

O,
unhappy Days

Richard: *"I feel underpaid and I want to ask for a raise, or else look for another job..."*

Jody: *"My relationship is going down the tubes. I need to learn to communicate more effectively..."*

Nicky: *"I am out of shape. I want to join a gym..."*

Neil: *"I am so high-strung, I need to learn to relax..."*

If I am to walk away with one conclusion after years of counselling and coaching in a private practice, it would be that most of us are well aware of our personal issues, and quite clear on what we should be doing to better our situations.

We usually have the **common sense** and **insight** required to identify our **needs** and **wants,** and to figure out our options and the steps we have to take, in order to lead more balanced and happier lives. Granted, coming to conclusions takes time. Sometimes we have to hear ourselves say things out loud. Other times we need some guidance or reassurance, a gentle probing, or one more "wake-up call" before we get the picture. What it comes down to, however, is that we are rarely incapable of doing our own groundwork.

The question then remains:
If most of us have enough wit to not only recognize our problems or concerns, but indeed come up with viable ways of solving our personal issues, then why are so many of us struggling?
The answer is really quite simple:

Because we procrastinate !!

I am convinced that only a small percentage of our personal discontent is due to real problems or true misfortune.
The lion's share of our dismay, we **create, maintain,** or even **aggravate,** as we **procrastinate**.
We delay, or refrain from, putting our common sense and insight into action.

That is why so many of us are struggling.

•2•

No Gain
without Pain

Our common sense tells us we need to go back to school if we ever want to get away from working menial or dead-end jobs. Our insight tells us we have to spend more quality time with the kids. Our persistent belly aches tell us it's time to see a doctor. Why do we linger, when push comes to shove? Why do we hesitate, when it comes time to take care of our needs and wants?

With every need, want, wish, hope, or dream come one or more **sacrifices**. Think about it:

♦ We have a need to go back to school. In order to do that successfully, we have to let go of certain things, such as free time, a wad of money, or maybe our reservations about our abilities.

♦ We dream of starting our own business. That means we may have to give up the security of a steady job elsewhere, and possibly face our fear of failing.

- We want to lose weight. In return we have to start eating sensibly and be willing to submit ourselves to strenuous physical activity. We may also have to face the reasons for our overeating, or overcome our qualms about wearing spandex.
- We wish to get out of our marriage. For that we may have to come to terms with the fact that we have failed at wedded bliss, perhaps we have to rise above our fear of being alone, maybe we have to let go of some guilt or shame, or possibly part with a certain lifestyle.

Be it changing a nappy or changing the world : no matter how pressing the need or want, or how strong the desire or dream, if we are **not willing** or **able** to make the **sacrifices** that come along with it, yet are **not prepared** to **admit** to this, **nor capable of letting go** of our **need or want,** then the real trouble begins: we are stuck, and well on our way to becoming a **procrastinator.**

Procrastination is a behaviour that causes us to **neglect** our needs and wants, and **betray** the principles and values that are important to us. It keeps us from realizing our hopes and dreams. It **undermines** the steps we know we should be taking in order to make things right or more enjoyable for us.

.3.

Defining Procrastination

Mike: *"Can I let you know later?"*

Christi: *"It's when we're all talk and no action."*

Vince: *"I've been a member of Procrastinators Anonymous for a few months now. I'll be going to my first meeting soon."*

Kathie: *"It's when I put off doing my taxes until the last minute."*

While virtually all of us perceive procrastination as something negative or unpleasant, and are eager to share our experiences, most of us prefer to identify procrastination by example or some form of satire, rather than definition. Yes, procrastination has something to do with "later", "no action", "soon", and "putting things off", but not every time we cause delay or refrain from taking further steps, are we procrastinating.

Since procrastination is so widespread and our experiences so diverse, we have to find some common ground on which we can do our work.

For this reason we will define procrastination as follows:

To Procrastinate:

to delay,
postpone,
or put off

Needlessly

Sometimes we have good reason to postpone or even abandon our chores, duties, needs and wants. They may, for instance, be somewhat unrealistic, or it just doesn't seem right or responsible to pursue them at that particular time. We reschedule our dentist appointment because we are truly sick with the flu. We refrain from signing a contract because we have our reservations about what we read in the fine print. We delay a presentation, because we need to do more research before we can dazzle a prospective client. In these types of instances we have just motive; the delay we create is not needless, and so we are not procrastinating.

The act of procrastination takes form when we postpone or abandon our needs and wants, not by stating our true motives, but by making up **excuses**:

♦ We mean to fix the fence, but instead of saying we don't know how to do it, we say can't find our tools.
♦ We want to ask our boss for a raise, but instead of admitting we are scared, we say now is not the right time.
♦ We know we have a drinking problem, but instead of admitting we have no control over the situation, we maintain it isn't that bad.

Since delay and cancellation due to procrastination is based on fibs and fabrications, it is, per definition, **unnecessary**.
What's more, procrastination only complicates things as it covers up the **real reasons** behind our dragging our heels: these of course being the various **sacrifices** we face in the pursuit of our need or want, and which we are reluctant to make - and admit to - at the time.

.4.

Why we can't handle the Truth

Why do we prefer to tell lies, or half-truths, and cause needless delay, while subsequently prolonging our suffering, when the truth can set us free to overcome our reservations and deal with our needs and wants once and for all?

We can't speak the truth because...

Exposing the real reasons for our lingering can:
- leave us feeling **vulnerable**
- hurt our **ego**
- threaten our **reputation**

The truth lying with the sacrifices, on closer inspection it becomes clear that they all **say something** about our **person**; something we may not necessarily be proud of, or that (we believe) can be construed as a character flaw or personal weakness.

Meet Sally:

Sally recently moved into town and wants to meet new people. The price she has to pay is that she overcomes her shyness. Admission to timidness, however, leaves Sally feeling exposed and open to ridicule. Unable to bear this, she resorts to excuse by proclaiming she really is too busy with other matters for an active social life.

Meet Cal:

Cal's bad temper has ruined several love relationships. Deep down, he knows he needs to learn to control himself. To do so, he has to first overcome his reluctance to openly admit he has problems containing his anger. Unwilling to make this sacrifice, Cal chooses to downplay his need by telling himself the other parties "deserved" his wrath.

Both Sally and Cal may have saved face by not mentioning the **unmentionable**, but where has it really gotten them?

Absolutely nowhere...

.5.

Why we should take Note

Although Sally may have eluded possible embarrassment, avoiding the truth only hinders her in dealing with her self-consciousness, and consequently her need to meet new people.

Cal's excuse provides him with instant relief (and enables him to sleep at night). Regrettably, a short time later his temper gets him in hot water again, and his need to seek anger management resurfaces.

Procrastination is a behaviour that allows us to **escape reality** and **avoid** the issues we should be dealing with in order to meet our need or want. Since it usually doesn't take us very long to come up with an excuse, it is also **instantly gratifying**, making it all the more tempting to resort to this behaviour. Unfortunately, the relief is usually **short-lived** and only lasts until the next time we are reminded of our need or want. Procrastination puts us in a **vicious circle**, allowing history to repeat itself over and over until we either decide to permanently *abandon* our need, or *take care* of our need by overcoming our hesitation about making the sacrifices. Since giving up a need is not always an option, (e.g. Sally would end up feeling very lonely. Cal would end up isolated and potentially in serious trouble), the only thing we can do is face our demons, or procrastinate.

Decisions, decisions…

We **wonder** and **worry** about the possible sacrifices we have to make in order to meet our need or want. If the emotions leading up to our lingering are not **tormenting** enough, then the feelings forthcoming from our humming and hawing are sure to keep us awake at night.

When we procrastinate we are basically looking away, and while we may manage to kid our surroundings (at least for a little while), we can't help but soon **feel bad** anyway, because we are certainly not fooling ourselves. Deep down we know we are **excusing** ourselves. We know we are being **indecisive**. We know we are not making any **progress**, and ultimately, we can't help but sense a **lack of control** over our personal welfare.

Fear, anger, frustration, sadness, guilt, shame, anxiety, hopelessness, and desperation are some sensations which may **plague** and **preoccupy** us as a result of our inability to take care of our needs and wants.

Sometimes these strong feelings turn out to be the extra bit of push, or motivation, we need to commence action after all. If this doesn't happen, however, and we remain stuck with a potentially **hefty burden of unaddressed negative emotions**, these will eventually, and without a doubt, come out sideways and give rise to headaches, ulcers, rashes, insomnia, high blood pressure, heart problems, stroke and many other **physical maladies.**

Bottled up feelings can drive us to drink, do drugs or engage in other **ill behaviours** in an effort to self-medicate and (temporarily) numb our suffering.

Chronic procrastination can in time also bring about **mental illness,** such as general anxiety or depression. It can also **significantly lower** our **sense of worth** and **self-confidence.**

But wait, there is more…

Procrastinate often enough and we **program our brain** as that being the preferable reaction to challenge or hardship, as such creating a **habit.** Once a habit is in place, it is hard to break. This phenomena works to our advantage if a habit happens to be a good one, but can be rather awful if the routine is a bad one. To break a bad habit, you see, we need **extra willpower**, something many lally-gaggers already have a lack of to begin with.

Obviously, not all needs and wants have to be met in order for us to live happy and meaningful lives. We deal with possible disappointment every day and then we get on with it.

Certain requirements and wishes, however, such as the need for friendship or love, the desire to be self-sufficient, or the yearning for an education, are too important to downplay or ignore. Chronically neglecting these types of needs and wants can have a **tremendous negative impact** on our general **well-being** and our **outlook on life**.

All of the above goes to show that while procrastination may at first seem like a decent solution, it only becomes part of our problems. This utterly **self-defeating** behaviour puts us in a **downward spiral** that only aggravates and prolongs our suffering in the long run and keeps us from doing the things we probably should have been doing in the first place.

Part II

The Origins of our Needs and Wants:

√ Nature
√ Nurture
√ Progress
√ The Sum of it all

W hat makes us want to do such things as earn a living, maintain a home, cook a meal, find a mate, have kids, build roads, search for cures, visit friends and family, go to church, climb a rock face, be unfaithful, pay our bills, volunteer...? Where do our needs and wants come from, or in other words: what drives us to do the things we do and potentially procrastinate about?

The answer to this question lies with the combination of three mighty forces, these being:

1. Nature

2. Nurture

3. Progress

Let's explore each of these powerhouses a bit further:

• Nature •

Nature's number one intention is to maintain life, including human life. In order to enhance our chances of survival she hard-wired virtually all of us with two primal, yet very powerful drives:

√   Make yourself **feel safe**

and then

√   make yourself **feel good**

This translates into us having to meet and satisfy certain fundamentals, the sum of which adds up to be our primary needs and desires. These are:

√ Physical, mental and emotional Health

We need to be able to count on body and mind so we can take care of ourselves and our loved ones.

√ Nourishment

We need food and drink to promote health and remain energized.

√ Shelter and territory

We need a place that safeguards us from severe weather and possible intruders.

√ Belonging

We are social creatures and feel safer and stronger in a group, so we need friends, family and other social and spiritual systems.

√ Love/mate

In order for our genes to survive we need to mate and bear offspring.

√ Fun

We will treasure and protect a life that we find enjoyable, and so having fun along the way further improves our odds of continued existence.

√ Curiosity

We will embrace a life that is stimulating and meaningful, and while curiosity may kill a cat or two, it generally drives us to explore, learn, ask questions, seek answers, go forward and possibly become the best we can be in every aspect of our life, allowing us to not only survive, but indeed to thrive.

While these basic needs and wants are pretty much universal for human kind, from this point forward Nature becomes more personal by instilling each of us with a distinct and individual blueprint:

√ Genetics

Our genes don't just determine our physical aspects such as eye colour, shoe size, and basic constitution, or make us more or less susceptible to conditions such as obesity, diabetes, or dyslexia, they can also instill us with certain personality traits or characteristics such as a shyness, anxiety, optimism, leadership, and aggressiveness, all of which will influence what we look for in life and how we go about meeting our needs and wants

There was a time in history when our needs and wants were pretty straight forward. When contentment was the sum of a full belly, being warm and dry, in the midst of loved ones and other familiar faces, with some stimulation and relaxation, and not too many bodily aches to give us grief, all the while being guided and protected by an optimistic, be it somewhat aggressive, but definitely natural-born Leader.

Happy Cavers

What happened? Homo Sapiens, that's what happened...

• Nurture •

From the day we are born, Nature and Nurture begin a complex interrelationship as they lay the groundwork for our future secondary needs and wants, as well as our (perceived) abilities to meet them.

The hands that rock our cradle and the social systems we are part of as we grow up, will heavily influence the outcome of our predispositions, the patterns, habits, traits and behaviours we form, the values we live by, and the roles we take on.

The Making of our Psychological Make-up:

As we grow, we not only need to learn such things as walk and talk, but also experience and master certain mental and emotional tasks. This process and its outcome will determine in what light we will see ourselves, others, and the world around us; it will also greatly affect what life choices we will make, and how we go about making them.

As infants we are utterly helpless creatures and in dire need of a loving and trustworthy environment that supplies us with consistent care, warmth, physical and emotional nurturing. It is under these circumstances that we can learn to put basic **trust** in others, which enables us to **bond**, to **nurture** and **be nurtured**. In the mean time we also learn that the world around us is a trustworthy and safe enough place to live in, which helps us gain a **positive outlook on life and the future.**

Over time we not only become more physically independent, but also begin the huge task of **slowly separating** emotionally from our primary caregivers. They help us in this process by allowing us to be curious and explore our environment, by letting us try things out for ourselves, by initiating activities and gently urging us to see them through, while guiding us in the right direction by exhibiting good and consistent example, and setting healthy limits for us.

Our growing **independence** creates a sense of **trust in ourselves** and our **abilities,** as well as an awareness of the fact that we can generally and eventually solve most of our own problems and **influence** our own **destiny**.

As we live and learn, we slowly replace our caregivers' limit setting by our own "encourage-and discourage-mechanism" in the form of **healthy shame, doubt** and **guilt**. In plain words: we develop a conscience, a moral sense that safeguards us from getting hurt, or hurting others and possibly facing rejection by our social environment.

Healthy shame will keep us from, for instance, picking our nose in public, producing shoddy work, or being in other ways objectionable or offensive in the eyes of our fellow man.

Healthy doubt makes us think twice before we put ourselves or others in dicey situations, such fixing the car brakes ourselves without proper training, or taking on too risky business ventures.

Guilt will keep most of us from writing bad cheques, slashing our ex's tires, or otherwise doing things which are considered wrong or hurtful within our communities.

Healthy shame, doubt, and guilt teach us how to behave ourselves and treat others in so we may become **responsible** and **socially acceptable** members of society; they eventually also determine how we allow others to treat us as we begin to form our **boundaries**.

While we work on our independence, our caregivers and our growing social circle (e.g. school, soccer club, church, neighbourhood) each set demands and expectations. By encouraging us in a safe and gentle manner to meet these set norms, we develop **willpower, self-control,** and a sense of **competence**, which in turn nurture our **self-esteem** or **self-worth.**

By now we have a basic trust in people, the world around us, our abilities, and ourselves. We are working on our healthy independence, and are well on our way to developing morals in terms of what is right and what is wrong. We have moved from self-centered to a more social thinking through practising to play and work nice with others. Our role models have been nurturing and respectful, they believe in us and made us believe in ourselves. All of the above gives us a sense of **security** and **confidence**. We start to believe in our own **personal power** and in our ability to **nurture** and **take care of ourselves.**

Believing in our own person enables us to integrate our various **roles** of son or daughter, sibling, parent, friend, employee, lover, and so on, into one identity.

I'm a bitch, I'm a lover, I'm a child, I'm a a mother. I'm a sinner, I'm a saint...

song by Meredith Brooks

We can do this successfully by setting clear boundaries for each of these roles. We are children to our parents. We are parents to our children. We are employees to our employers. We are lovers to our partners. We know the do's, and the taboo's within the various roles. The boundaries are not blurred and we don't try to be everything for everybody. We can safely fit all our roles into one identity.

Identifying who and what we are results in us looking for a **sense of purpose**. We want to find out what our place is within the social system, and what we want to do with our lives.

When we are young we live mostly by our parents' morals and values. As we mature, get a mind of our own, and actively begin to search for our niche in life, we often start to **rethink the set of standards we grew up with**, and slowly begin the process of adjusting or replacing them with values that are now worthwhile and important to us, and by which we want to live our life.

The values we hold in high regard, combined with the roles we choose to play (e.g. student, friend, amateur golfer), we happen to fall into (e.g. unplanned parenthood, flu sufferer) or consciously wish to take on in the future (e.g. entrepreneur, lover, amateur golfer extraordinaire), determine our secondary needs and wants.

This is providing all goes well...

In a perfect world we would all be born with great genes. We would grow up in fine families, free of violence, addictions, mental illness, or extreme poverty.

We would be surrounded and supported by social systems that would help us master the developmental tasks successfully by the time we fly the parental coop. We would grow up to be well-balanced individuals: trusting, yet not gullible. Confident, yet not reckless. Responsible, but by no means a doormat. And so on and so forth.

We would have been raised equally, despite us being different from our siblings, or our order of birth. Our environment would even have picked up on our predisposed shyness and helped us outgrow it. They would have dealt with our aggressive tendencies by encouraging us to find positive outlets for it, such as in sports or other areas that promote healthy competition.

With all this good stuff in place we can now, as adults, consciously choose the roles we want to play in life and live them by the values that are important to us, enabling us to all live meaningful and uncomplicated lives.

Alas, in reality it is rarely so...

The fact remains that most of us end up missing, or not successfully completing, at least one or more developmental phases while growing up, leaving us scarred or fragile in particular areas of our psyche.

It is there, at the level(s) of wounding, where our needs and wants often not only become most **pressing** and **complex**, but also potentially **warped**.

Emotional injuries can be very powerful and can easily - and unfortunately often will - get the better of us. Our weaknesses can cause us to leave our going standards, values and common sense in the dust and lead us to believe and do all kinds of foolish things. They can create an array of additional problems for us, and since we typically and most often tend to procrastinate around matters pertaining to our emotional scars and weaknesses, our problems are often maintained and even aggravated by the act of needless delay. Let's clarify this with an example:

Meet Luke:

Luke is a young man who, like most everyone else, has a primary need to love and be loved.

Earlier life experiences, however, taught him that getting attached to someone generally meant getting hurt down the line, so over time attachment, or the ability to bond, became Luke's level of wounding.

As an adult he still feels the inborn need for love and belonging, but in his effort to stay away from the pain that comes with eventual rejection or break-up - and in Luke's mind this is inevitable - he now avoids getting too close to any one girlfriend he has at the time, making emotional distance a (subconscious, yet clearly unfavourable) secondary need to love.

Luke's need for emotional distance calls for certain, mostly unpleasant beliefs and behaviours. Luke often withdraws and his girlfriend complains he is perpetually vague about his true thoughts and feelings. Also, when the pressure goes up, Luke has a tendency to take off. Last week he "disappeared" for two days after a disagreement with his girlfriend, leaving her so upset, she almost broke it off with him.

Since Luke's love relationship lacks true commitment and emotional intimacy, it is rather volatile, making it all the harder for the lovers to ever become closer and find safety within the relationship.

All Luke really wants is lasting love and he is well-aware his ill behaviours are not helping his situation. He knows he needs learn to be more open and honest, but as long as Luke allows his weaknesses to overrule his common sense, he, as well as his girlfriend, will remain in a constant state of hesitation.

But wait, since we often operate on both sides of the emotional spectrum the opposite can also happen:

> Over the years Luke has become so afraid of being "dumped", that in his quest to feel safe and good (or less bad) in the love department, he now virtually latches on to the person of his affection, making emotional enmeshment a (subconscious, yet again unfavourable) secondary need to love. Since Luke is so needy of this relationship he not only risks pushing away his girlfriend with his smothering ways, he also is more prone to, and more likely to put up with, otherwise intolerable behaviours from his partner, triggering more warped needs such as for constant reassurance, obsessing, or even stalking.
>
> Knowing deep down that the way the relationship is going is not good for him, Luke feels the need to change or to get out all together, yet may hesitate and procrastinate because, as with everything in life, there is no guarantee that change will give Luke the result he seeks, and so rather than taking a risk, Luke holds on to what little he has.
>
> A few stormy months later his girlfriend breaks it off with Luke, stating his behaviours are suffocating her.

Since Luke is not dealing with his emotional injuries, there is a good chance Luke will find himself confronting the same warped secondary needs and wants, and subsequently run into the same difficulties in future love relationship, as he did in previous ones. While history keeps on repeating itself Luke becomes more and more convinced that love always hurts, making his wounds even deeper and his love life ever more problematic.

Please take note that completion of the developmental tasks are relative to each aspect of life, and that the levels of success or failure can differ from the one area one to the next.

A love-deprived child may, for example, find a safe haven and gain positive experiences in working for the school newspaper or becoming a candystriper at the local hosital. The result may be that later in life this person, while maybe insecure at love, can turn out to become a confident worker.

This also explains why problems, and procrastination, often seem to hit certain aspects of our life more frequently and persistently than other areas.

Next time you run into that person that exudes confidence, make sure you get the the whole picture...

I see you are loyal to your wife and friends, but you cheat on your taxes.
You are a successful businessman, but you're hopeless at relaxing and having fun.

Then, there are the Times we live in, that are ever a'changing...

• Progress •

There was a day way back when we didn't consider head lice or cholesterol to be health issues, running water to be a must, TV nor Pokémon cards to be basic necessities, or a philandering partner to be a major problem.

We did however feel the need at one time to have holes drilled in our head to release alleged demons, to burn witches at the stake, and gather to listen to the town crier.

Changing times and progress have created and dissolved, and will continue to create and dissolve, many secondary needs and wants.

Most of these requirements and wishes are relatively trivial and will come and go as they serve to convenience us, but are not essential for our survival.

Some needs and wants however, such as for hospitals, sewer systems, garbage disposal, power plants, roads, but also needs for law and order, censuses, and so on, have over time become more or less pertinent to our continued welfare and existence. While these are fairly new needs and wants, nowadays we'd be in big trouble without them, (but don't be surprised if these too become obsolete one day).

The remote!
I can't find the remote!
I am doomed! .

• The Sum of it all •

Nature, providing us with basic needs and certain genetic predispositions, and Nurture moulding us into individuals with distinct personalities and preferences, combined with the times and circumstances we live in, determine our needs and wants.

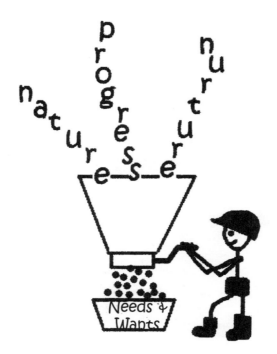

Now that we know where our needs and wants come from, and why we may procrastinate about meeting them, it is time to have a look at the main reasons behind our needless day.

Part III

The
Unmentionables

or

the real Reasons behind our Dragging Heels

Reason 1: Fear

Meet Lisa:

Frank and Lisa met in College. When Lisa got pregnant, they decided to get married and soon Lisa dropped out to stay at home and raise their child. Before long she got pregnant again. Years pass and as the children become more independent Lisa has a growing desire to go back to college. Frank thinks it's a great idea, so a couple of weeks later Lisa walks into the college to pick up an application, when she is consumed by certain thoughts and expectations:

"What if I can't keep up?" "The courses have changed so much, I may not have what it takes anymore."
What if I am unsuccessful; what kind of example will I be to the kids?"

As she waits in line, she suddenly remembers she needs to pick up Frank's shirts. *"I better do that right now, before the dry-cleaner closes. I can go back to the college some other day."* Lisa runs for the door - without the application.

Mama Nature instilled us with apprehension for good reason: so we may stay out of - in the olden days particularly physical - harms way to see the sun come up for yet another day. This is why most of us do not really like risk taking. Nowadays however, our **Fear of Failure** is not so much about making a mistake and potentially losing life or limb anymore, as it is about erring and possibly losing face. Emotional threat is often harder to admit to than physical intimidation, and so rather than being honest and open about it, which would allow us to deal with it, we choose to deny it and cover it up with excuses.

Meet Pamela:

Pamela works for a prestigious marketing agency as the assistant to one of the account executives. Over the years she has helped her boss secure major accounts with her fresh ideas and creative input. Her boss, to whom Pamela's work and abilities did not go unnoticed, has suggested numerous times she apply for the junior account executive positions that become available at the agency from time to time. However keen on the idea herself, Pamela always seems to miss the deadline or find some outlandish reason why she can't apply a that time. The one time she did apply, she phoned to cancel the third and final interview, stating her mom had come down with the flu and that she was taking a couple of weeks off to visit and take care of her.

We may believe for some reason or another that we do not deserve it. We may believe for some reason or another that others believe we do not deserve it. We may fear ridicule, envy, or wrath. We may think we are unable to handle the pressures that come with achievement, such as more responsibility, putting in the extra time, meeting certain expectations, or the need to continue to do well.

Accomplishment and prosperity, however desirable, can be very intimidating for some of us, and our **Fear of Success** can lead us to (subconsciously) undermine our every effort to get ahead.

Meet Joey:
Joey is a young, single, and healthy man, and a carpenter by trade. He can be found in the local pub every night, where he can't seem to stop complaining about the small town he lives in: how boring it is, how there is not enough work, and how he will soon leave for the big and prosperous city.
Joey has been talking about his move for five years now. He still lives in the small town. He still visits the same local watering hole every night. He still is miserable.

As some of us are engulfed by thoughts of potential fiasco or triumph, others can't seem to get started or see things through because the pressure of simply not knowing what may or may not come their way, becomes too overwhelming.
We generally to not take lightly to change since it usually invoves risk. **Fear of the unknown or unpredictable** may make us choose to stay in bad, but familiar and predictable situations, rather than face an uncertain future.

Even though angst may not be the driving force behind us not doing the laundry, fear is one of the more prominent causes of us not pursuing our dreams or making desired changes. Unfortunately, many a time our fears are ungrounded as they are all too often based on mistaken beliefs and figments of our imagination, causing us to needlessly waste yet another wish or dream.

To what extent we fear failure, success, or the unpredictable has a lot to do with the level of **trust** and **confidence** we have in ourselves and our abilities, as well as how we feel about others and the world we live in, since these factors will largely determine how risky we find something, and how **doubtful** or **optimistic** we are about overcoming challenge.

Rings a bell? If so:

√ **Admit** it, say it out loud:
"I'm scared",
Then, try to be more specific:
"I fear failure",
"I fear success", or
"I fear the unknown".

√ Proceed with writing down point wise everything you are really worried about, e.g.
- *"I fear failure because I'm not sure if I can keep up with my courses."* (rational concern)
- *"My colleagues will think I've slept my way to the top."* (irrational concern)
- *"I am afraid of burning my bridges."* (could be a rational concern)
- *"I'll never make it."* (probably an irrational concern)

√ Writing things down frees our mind of worrisome thoughts, making it more readily available to search for sulutions. Since we omit the hoopla and excuses and are left with the bare facts, the actual reasons also tend to become less intimidating and more **manageable**. What's more, as we see before us and in writing what is holding us back, it frequently dawns on us that our fears and concerns are a tad silly or irrational.

√ Separate rational from irrational concerns.
Irrational concerns can often be identified by their:
- **rigid** (absolutes, never, always, must, have to),
- **over-reactive** (e.g. failing is unforgivable, not being liked is devastating), or
- **self-berating** (e.g. I'm not deserving, I'm not smart enough) characteristics.

√ If you sense your concerns are rational, check if your need or want is **feasible** in the first place. Sometimes we can set unrealistic goals, or have excessively high expectations.

√ If you feel your need or want is attainable, maybe all it needs is some **readjusting** in order for you to get going:
- ♦ *"I could start out with a lighter course load and see how it goes."*
- ♦ *"The only sure thing is that there are no guarantees. Things may go differently than planned or hoped, but will nonetheless work out fine."*

√ Give your irrational concerns a **voice-over,** e.g.:
- ♦ *"I know I worked hard to get where I am. I deserve this promotion, it doesn't matter what other people think."*
- ♦ *Nonsense, I can make it if I set my mind to it; where there is a will there is a way."*

√ Do your **research** and **preparation.**
This will help you reduce the risk, make things more manageable, as well as lower your anxiety levels.

√ Set **a clear main goal**.
Be precise about what it is you want to attain, and know your finish line.
Research has shown that karate students partaking in push-ups generally performed better if they were told to do a certain number, rather than told to do push-ups for an unspecified amount of time.
Yes, it is a psychological thing, but the fact remains we tend to fare better when we know more or less what we are up against.
"Sales have to go up", is a start, but a clearer goal would be: *"I want a 20% increase in sales from last year"*.

√ Once you have a clear main goal, **set sub-goals** by figuring out what steps you need to take in order to realize your main goal.

Divvy-ing up your main goal into sub-goals not only tends to make things less overwhelming, but also gives you a starting point and usually some freedom of choice as to where to begin. An example:

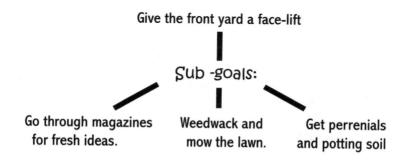

Main Goal:

Give the front yard a face-lift

Sub -goals:

| Go through magazines for fresh ideas. | Weedwack and mow the lawn. | Get perrenials and potting soil |

√ Get the **momentum** going.

Pick a sub-goal, any sub-goal, and start! You will notice that once you get going it usually becomes easier to keep things in motion.

√ Try to settle into a routine that works for you.

√ Be prepared to face a certain amount of challenge, as there really is no such thing as a risk-free or effortless endeavour.

√ Allow yourself to live and learn, it is natural to make mistakes along the way. Dust yourself off and get back in the saddle.

√ Instead of fearing the unknown, treasure the fact that life is unpredictable. After all, that is what makes it interesting!

Reason 2: Lack of meaning

Meet Marian:

Hubby is off to work, the kids are on their way to school and Marian has the house to herself.

She sits at the kitchen table and a heavy sigh escapes her as she looks around: the place is a mess, ... again. Sometimes she wonders why she even bothers cleaning. Two hours later Marian finds herself on the couch watching the soaps on TV, the house still in disarray.

We scrub bathtubs, make beds, mop floors, or for that matter stand behind an assembly line, or file files and sharpen pencils in a dingy office, only to do it again a short time thereafter.

It is hard to get motivated if we **can't see the benefits** of fulfilling the task, the **gratification** we get from it is very **short lived**, or others, (or worse, we) have **no respect for the work** we do, which can leave us feeling disappointed, empty, exploited and resentful.

Part of feeling good about life and ourselves, is having a sense **usefulness** and **contribution**, a feeling that what we do matters and makes a difference. It is therefore important that, while we have to accept that certain jobs - significant or not - just need to get done, doing tasks we consider to be meaningless are to remain the exception rather than become the norm in our life.

Rings a bell? If so

√   **Admit** it.
    Let yourself hear you say it: *"This really sucks!"*

√   Find out exactly what makes it meaningless to you and change it if possible.

√   If others are part of the problem **talk** to them (e.g. have a heart to heart with the person who leaves the grubby ring in the bath tub every day).

√   **Accept necessary evils**, but make them more pleasurable by, for instance, playing background music, having someone else join in, or partaking in job sharing or chore rotation.

√   **Reward yourself** for a job well-done. Warm apple pie with whipped cream and a dash of Bailey's can really hit the spot after washing all the windows, (and may actually have someone else wish they had helped out. So line them up for next time!).

√   **Delegate!**

√   If you can afford it, **pay** someone to do it.

√   If it is your livelihood you find meaningless, seriously consider changing jobs, as most of them do not pay enough to justify being miserable eight hours a day.

√   If you really can't change the meaningless features in your life, at least find good outlets, such as warm friendships, or a wild hobby. This can help you put matters in perspective and find some **balance**, making things more bearable.

Reason 3: Inefficiency

Meet Ron:

Ron is in business for himself making marzipan flowers, which he sells to bakeries who use them for cake decoration.

Today was the day that Ron was supposed to send off some orders, but he will not get to that since he was unable to make marzipan flowers yesterday, because he didn't buy almonds the day before, because he wasn't aware he had run out.

Ron's disorganization gets to him sometimes, so much so that on occasion he just locks up and calls it a day.

We are running around aimlessly. We are busy, yet can't seem to get things done. Last things seem to come first, first things seem to pop up last. Supplies go missing. Responsibilities are forgotten. Appointments are missed.

To make a long story short: there is confusion abound and things just don't seem to run smoothly.

Disarray may be caused by overload, but can also be the result of **lack of structure**, and ouch... plain **bad management**! It can be very frustrating to sense we do not have things under control, and trying to dodge this uneasy feeling, we may avoid the tasks that are causing it, all together.

Rings a bell? If so

√ **Admit** you are a scatterbrain.

√ Accept that you need to change your ways, and that running away from things does not solve anything.

√ Why do things such as tools and appliances come with manuals?
Why do companies, however seemingly annoying, like to have their policies and job descriptions in place?
Why does Kraft Dinner come with cooking directions?
Exactly! To avoid chaos!
Not all of us are fond of red tape, administration, and paper trails, yet we have to admit they do serve a purpose.
If you find yourself regularly flustered, it may be time for you too, to sit down and **get organized** by **reviewing** and **prioritizing**, and jotting down some guidelines of your own.

√ Buy a good planner, get one of those funky electronic palm note pads (make sure to read the manual), write to-do lists, stock up on post-it notes.

√ Take a course in **time management** or **personal productivity**.

√ Know your **strengths** and **weaknesses**.
Some of us may for instance be hopeless with numbers, but masters at sales or closing deals. Find ways to strengthen your weaker areas. Otherwise focus on what you know and **accept your limitations**. The saying, *"do what you do best and pay for the rest,"* is not that outlandish, and may save you a lot of grief in the long run. So find someone to help you out in the areas you are not comfortable.

Reason 4: Inability to say No

Meet Sonny:

Father: *"Son, you're going to Law School".*
Sonny : *"But dad, I want to become a Forest Ranger!"*
Father: *"Nonsense, you're going to Law School!"*
Sonny : *"Yes dad".*

After graduating Sonny became a junior partner in his dad's Prestigious Law Firm and proceeded to work there

for seven long years. As time went on, Sonny grew more somber and withdrawn. He started taking long breaks during his workday, became negligent and forgetful toward his cases, and would phone in sick more and more often.

As children we live mainly by the needs, wants and values of our primary caregivers. With adulthood, comes the freedom to question and, if desired, adjust these standards.

Some of us however, particularly the ones raised in an overbearing, overly protective, controlling or rejecting environment, were not able to successfully complete this transition, and often continue to live life according to other people's expectations and wishes.

Inability to speak up for ourselves, or to say no, increases our chances to get stuck with roles and tasks we don't want, or are unable to do, in the first place. Resentment and possible overload can make it all the harder to get going.

Rings a bell? If so:

√ **Admit** you have a hard time saying no.

√ Ask yourself whom you are trying to **please** right now, at the **expense** of your own needs or wants?

√ Why are you trying to **appease** this person? What are you afraid of will happen if you turn down their request?

√ Is his or her approval at the expense of your needs a **fair trade**?
   If your answer is no, and you find yourself getting the short end often enough, then you will probably feel resentment. The ironic part of it all is that while you partaking in this charade to avoid other people's rejection or anger, you still have to deal with the wrath of someone you didn't count on: your own! You can't help but feel **angry and frustrated** with **yourself** for your inability to speak up for yourself. The worst part of this is that, unlike most other critics, your inner critic gets to come home with you; there to plague, pester, and give you emotionals beating to no end. What's more, he won't even let you get a good night's sleep.

√ **Boundaries** are what separate us physically and emotionally from others. They give us a sense of self, which allows us to feel safe within the roles we play, and enable us to make our own choices. During childhood, while treated fairly and with respect, we learn to recognize and protect our physical and emotional spaces, as well as respect the ones of others. If we do not learn to set healthy boundaries, we often end up unable to protect them as adults, making ourselves prone to living life on other people's terms, or otherwise be taken advantage of. While Sonny is Father's child, Father crossed the parent-child line by telling Sonny what career to choose. Since being a lawyer is not Sonny's choice, he struggles with an identity not his own, leaving him unhappy and unfulfilled.

√   While there is nothing wrong with doing someone a favour once in a while, next time you find yourself in a situation you feel someone is crossing "your" line and you really don't want them to, take a deep breath, muster all your courage, and speak up for yourself in a calm and collected way. Quite possibly, the reaction is not as negative as you would have expected it to be, since they too are probably aware they are "pushing it."

√   Know that **opposites attract**: people who regularly disrespect other people's space are often particularly drawn to individuals with weak boundaries. If you have a hard time speaking up for yourself, chances are you have your share of boundary-pokers routinely hanging around you. As you learn to set your limits, be prepared to deal with their resistance and manipulative behaviour, which they will without a doubt turn up a notch or two, in their efforts to sway you after all. The word here is **consistency:** no matter how big of a tantrum they throw, **stick to your Decision.** Once they figure out you are no longer an easy target, they'll go on to greener pastures. Yes you may lose a "friend" or two, but the ones you do lose over this, probably weren't much of a friend in the first place.

√   If you continue to be a "pushover", or if you persistently seem to offend people with your turndowns, maybe your technique needs fine-tuning. Either way, it may be wise to sign yourself up for a good **assertiveness course**, or at least make an effort to observe and learn from others who are more outspoken, and who's ways you look up to.

But wait, there is more to Sonny's story:

> Then one day Sonny transferred all his cases to a willing colleague, told his father he quit, and walked out the Prestigious Law door. "He'll be back", said Father. Everybody waited and waited, but Sonny did not return. Many trials later a post card arrived at Prestigious Law Firm. On the front was a beautiful mountain range. The back read:

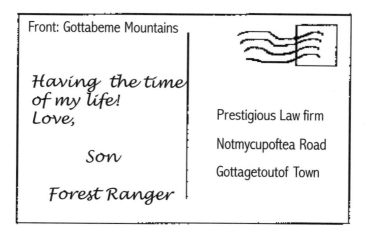

Front: Gottabeme Mountains

Having the time of my life!
Love,

Son

Forest Ranger

Prestigious Law firm

Notmycupoftea Road

Gottagetoutof Town

> When Father came out of his office and asked what all the commotion was about, the staff grew quiet and handed him the post card. Moments passed, everybody just stood there in fear and anticipation of Father's reaction.
> *"Well, son of a gun"*, Father finally said, *"I guess Sonny grew up." "Now, if you'll excuse me, I have a man to call and congratulate with his new position". Father closed the door behind him.*

√ Always remember: It is never too late to grow up, and start living life on your own terms. As the saying goes: some of the most beautiful flowers are late bloomers.

Reason 5: To avoid responsibility

Meet Jackie:
Jackie is in her early thirties and still lives with her parents. Apart from working a part-time job, she can usually be found hanging out with some friends at the local coffee shop. Since Jackie maintained she was broke again, her parents recently paid for her car repairs. Jackie never helps out around the house, and often forgets to feed or walk her dog, which has basically been adopted by her parents.

Once in a while her parents will ask Jackie when she plans to move out. "*As soon as I find a full-time job,*" she'll answer. When they inquire how the job search is going, Jackie tells them that "*there aren't any jobs worth applying for,*" or that she is "*waiting for the local economy to change*". In the mean time Jackie is often heard complaining about how "nagging" and "meddling" her parents are.

As a young and restless teenager with the classic "can't wait to get outta here" attitude, I did not understand my parents when they told me to: "*just enjoy your years with us, dear, since these will be the most worry-free years of your life.*" Naturally, they were right… again.

While flying the coop may be liberating, taking care of ones own needs and wants can from time to time also be quite overwhelming and worrisome. So much so, that some of us choose to remain, or become again, dependent on others, rather than take responsibility for our own well-being. Although being taken care of , may seem like a cushiony position to be in, in the long run it really isn't. As a dependent our needs and wants are left in the hands of others, leaving us **vulnerable** and more prone to **disappointment, bitterness** and **blame**.

Another reason why we shouldn't be in a dependent position as adults is that we basically remain, or fall back, in the child role, which clearly can not be good for our self-worth.

Unfortunately, even though we generally do not appreciate being branded a loser, freeloader, or the proverbial "mama's boy", for some this still seems easier to bear than the weight of responsibility.

Dependency has its definite drawbacks. On the other hand, being under someone else's wings undeniably comes with hidden advantages. We may, for instance, end up with more free time, less worry, or fewer bills.

Secondary gains can lead us to procrastinate about taking steps toward becoming independent adults. A state of being, that would make us feel better about ourselves and happier in the long run.

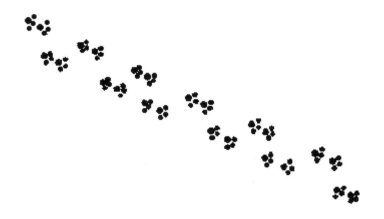

Rings a bell? If so:

√ **Admit** you are avoiding responsibility.

√ Why do you think you avoid responsibility? Could it be that you grew up in an environment that:
  ◆ depicted an overly cautious view of the world,
  ◆ encouraged dependency by being overly protective, or too eager to come to your rescue,
  ◆ discouraged you from exploring, and possibly making your own mistakes, or seeing things through,
  ◆ was overly critical and set excessively high standards, making nothing you did good enough, creating an air of "why bother".

√ Or could it be you are just:
  ◆ lazy (in that case read the next chapter).

√ While it is good to know what triggered your need to avoid responsibility, it should not become a crutch, nor should it stop you from bettering yourself.
You are an adult now and it is time to become more responsible, despite the scars your soul may carry. You are probably well aware of what you need to do.

√ So do it!

√ If the first thing that comes to mind is: *"I'm trying to,"* then answer this:
"Are you trying really, really hard, have you truly given it your best? Probably not. There are many roads that lead to Rome, maybe you are staring yourself blind on the wrong path. What else can you do?
A different approach is maybe all that's needed.

√ Beware of comebacks like *"I've tried everything"*, or the classic *"yes, but.."*, as they may be an indication that you are not ready to let go let go of the many **secondary gains** that come with dependency. Excuses and procrastination are a great way to sabotage your own efforts.

√ If you are undermining your own efforts, and you intend to keep doing this, at least **quit complaining** about what comes, or doesn't come, your way.

√ You have a choice. You can become **bitter** or **better**. If you do want things to change, then start acknowledging your true needs and wants and begin setting some goals.

√ If you want to become more responsible and fulfill your own needs and wants , but you need help doing so, by all means, find it. There is absolutely no shame in that. Talk to people that can help you on your way. Take a course. Find a coach. Do what you need to do.

√ Remember the first time you successfully tied your shoe laces on your own? Made you feel good, didn't it? The ability to do things yourself and take care of your own needs and wants, will do that to you. As an adult too, you will find that the sweetest gains and accomplishments are the ones that are truly your own.

Reason 6: Laziness

Meet Raymond:
The living room is scattered with dirty socks, empty beer bottles, knocked over ashtrays, and ground in potato chips. The kitchen sink is filled with foul smelling dishes. Kitty's litter box has not been attended to in days and God only knows what Raymond did in the bathroom.

Mark, Raymond's roomy, often complains to him about his untidiness, but to no avail. After hearing yet another, *"I'll get to it later,"* Mark can't take the disarray any longer and reaches for the yellow rubber gloves. Raymond can't help but feel a little pleased with himself as he peeks around the corner, while getting ready to watch the football game, and sees Mark working his way through a pile of dirty dishes.

Sometimes we lally-gag to get away with things, not because the responsibility is more than we can bear, but simply because we do not feel like **exerting** ourselves. While some of us lazybones are willing to suffer the consequences, (e.g. live in our own dirt), the true and somewhat more ingenious sloth has found a way to have his cake, eat it, and leave the mess too, by relying on the fact that when one dilly-dallies long enough,

52

someone else will usually and eventually pick up the slack. The difference between this type of loafing, and the previous one (Reason no.5: to avoid responsibility), lies in how we are left feeling about ourselves in the end. While the lazybones' self-worth is probably left fairly unaffected, the latter one suffers serious damage to his or her self-esteem in the long run. Given enough time, however, both are likely to experience some form of social disapproval.

Rings a bell? If so:

√ **Admit** you are feeling a tad lazy right now.

√ It's alright to feel like doing nothing once in a while. It's Nature's way of making sure we take a break from time to time, and **conserve our energy**.

√ Laziness as such is generally accepted, provided we have taken care of our immediate needs and obligations. If you find your surroundings are becoming annoyed or resentful towards you, it may be a sign you have fallen short in this matter, and that it is time to **smarten up**.

√ The TV show '*Survivor*' is a fine example of what tends to happen with members that don't carry their weight within the tribe: they get voted off real fast! Continue on your lazy way and chances are that one day you too, will become a **social outcast**.

√ If you don't want to eventually find yourself hanging on to the fringes of society, but you don't want to do your chores either, then consider this novel idea: **pay** others to do your dirty work, or better yet, make a **trade**, for instance, you cook, they clean.

Reason 7: Other obligations

Meet Jolene and Dave:
Jolene and Dave are married and have two children. They both work full-time and are in the midst of building a new addition to their house. Two nights a week Jolene goes to evening classes to upgrade her skills. Dave coaches little league on the weekends, and is the volunteer treasurer for the local museum. The rest of their time is spent with the children and doing projects around the house. Jolene and Dave also love to bike, and each spring the topic of taking a few weeks off to cycle around the country comes up, only to be shelved for yet another year.

We wait going back to school until the children are a little older. We shelve the dream of starting our own business until we are more financially secure. We postpone our outing to the zoo until the next long weekend.

Sometimes we have to put things off because of **other commitments** or **bad timing**. That's life and that's all right, as long as the other responsibilities do not create a prolonged imbalance in life, or become a source for resentment.

Traditional role division being a thing of the past, life may have become more enjoyable, but possibly also more hectic. This is because, even though we now have the freedom to let go of the traditional gender roles, we often choose not to. Instead we only add on new roles: women still do housework and raise children, but these days many of them also hold a paying job. Most men are still gainfully employed, but now also do housework and are involved in raising the children. While sharing roles may lighten the burden in certain areas of our life, overall it still requires more of our time.

Nowadays we want it all, and preferably all at the same time. As we juggle health, home, career, family, and numerous hobbies and interests we can end up spreading ourselves too thin. Procrastination due to **conflicting roles** may be a sign we should **slow down**, or at least **review** and **reprioritize** our roles.
Funny, how exception proves the rule, because this may well be one of the few times that our procrastinating turns out to be a good thing: In this case it keeps us from pursuing everything at once, thus preventing possible burnout.

Rings a bell? If so

√ **Admit** you have a busy lifestyle and that your roles may be in conflict.

√ Make a list of the main roles you are playing, or *wish* to play, right now. Check the (particularly *quality*) time you spend on each of them.

Roles	not enough	Enough	too much
homemaker		✓	
mother	✓		
wife		✓	
traveller	✓		
athlete	✓		
artist	✓		
Scientist	✓		
clinician			✓
finances	✓		✓
family	✓		
admin			✓
reader wash			✓

Examples of Roles:

Male/Female
Son/Daughter
Brother/Sister
Family member
Parent
Friend
Health conscious person
Excessive eater/drinker
Hetero/bi/homosexual
Spouse/lover
Bachelor/rette
Religious/spiritual person
Provider
Colleague
Volunteer
Student
People Pleaser
Doormat
Bride's maid
Renter/ home owner
Homemaker
Environmentalist
Soccer coach
Golfer
Traveler
Home renovator
Organizer
Chef extraordinaire
Pet owner

√ As you see before you, on paper, where your efforts lie and how you spend your time, it becomes easier to figure out what changes you may have to make in order to lead a happier or more balanced life.

√ Check to see if you are setting enough time aside for each of the various aspects in life:

- ◆ Health (physical, mental, emotional)
- ◆ Nourishment } (Nowadays, these translate into
- ◆ Shelter   work and finances)
- ◆ Belonging (friends, family, social and spiritual systems)
- ◆ Love/mate
- ◆ Fun
- ◆ Curiosity (anything you do to experience and learn)

The more aspects we actively pursue, providing we don't overdo it - the more balanced we feel, and less vulnerable we are, should one or (goodness forbid) more aspects suddenly fall away or be negatively affected.

A person suffering from the flu (health), who has a soft blanket to keep him warm (shelter) and can sip on a cup of chicken noodle soup (nourishment), which was prepared by someone who cares (love and belonging), will probably feel less miserable and possibly heal faster, than a flu sufferer who doesn't have all these aspects in place.

While this is just a silly example, the fact remains we are usually better able to deal with loss, challenge, or misfortune, no matter what calibre, if we have other aspects in place to fall back on and find comfort in.

√ What can you do to to feel good and safe in every aspect of your life? _____

_____

_____

_____

_____

_____

_____

Reason 8: Lack of Know-how

Meet Darlene:

Darlene is a secretary at an insurance company and her boss has asked her to duplicate a document.

Standing in front of the copy machine she examines the pale reproduction it just spat out, and concludes the ink cartridge needs refilling. She opens the front of the copy machine, has a glance at the insides, and overwhelmed by its technical marvel, quickly closes it again. Clueless and therefore copy-less, she walks back to her desk and notices it is coffee time. "*I'll deal with it after my break*". Later, when her boss asks her for the copy, she tells her the phone has kept her busy, and that she will get it to her as soon as possible. In the mean time Darlene is anxiously keeping an eye on the copy machine, hoping that someone else using it, will refill the cartridge and solve her dilemma.

This is classic and all too common grounds for procrastination: we have a job to do, but don't know how to do it, or run into glitches we don't know how to solve, causing us to push the task at hand to the backburner.

Rings a bell? If so

√ **Admit** you lack the know-how.

√ While difficult tasks can intimidate the best of us, in every day life it is particularly the **unwilling, the insecure,** or the individuals with somewhat **fragile egos** who end up procrastinating.
♦ Sometimes we simply **don't feel like** putting in the extra effort to do some research and to get informed, so we can complete the task after all.
♦ Other times it a the **lack of confidence** in our own abilities to learn, problem-solve, and overcome, that causes us to hesitate.
♦ Occasionally it is our **self-consciousness** that gets in the way of progress. For some of us it is very hard to admit inability and powerlessness, let alone let someone in on that dirty little secret by asking for help.

√ If it is **apathy** that holding you back:
To avoid needless repetition, please refer to Reason 2 (Lack of meaning), Reason 6 (laziness) and Reason 11 (Boredom).

√ If you **lack the confidence**:
As children we learn to believe in ourselves, and our abilities:
♦ by being curious,
♦ by exploring,
♦ by making mistakes and learning from them,
♦ by seeing things through,
♦ by being under the watchful eye of nurturing, encouraging, yet limit setting caregivers.
If all goes well and with time, we eventually build a confidence that is no longer determined by what we can or can not do, but based on a general belief in ourselves that

we can accomplish and solve pretty much anything that comes our way by setting our mind to it. Once this type of confidence is cemented in place, it is hard to topple. Unfortunately, not all of us were given the luxury of a confidence building childhood. If this applies to you, then you need to learn now what you missed then. You do that with the same basics in mind: by being curious, by exploring, by learning, and allowing yourself to make mistakes, while insisting on finishing what you start, through practising determination, resilience, and problem solving.

That said; don't forget to be your own healthy limit setter. Please don't go on to rewire your house, just because you believe you can, or think you should be able to. Certain things are still best left to professionals.

√ If it is a matter of **ego**:
Particularly the perfectionists and the more controlling personalities among us, will have a hard time admitting to the fact that they too can be left baffled.

Growing up in an environment that was impatient, overly critical, controlling, or expected way too much of them as children, they now want to forever do things "the right way" and maintain everyone's approval, so as to avoid falling prey to criticism again.

If this is you, please lighten up and quit being so hard on yourself. You are a grownup now; an individual in your own right, who no longer needs to please anybody, or maintain anyone's approval, in order to feel worthy as a person.

Really, no one will think less of you when you ask for help, and the one's that do frown upon your humility..., well, stuff 'em, and let it be their problem.

You are human, and you too are entitled to not know, to be overwhelmed, to make mistakes, or to be in need of help from time to time.

Reason 9: Fatigue

Kim's Story:
Kim was up with her sick child for most of the night. In the morning, she hits the snooze button once too often, and ends up late for work. *"This traffic, I tell ya, it's getting worse by the day!"* she fibs, when she sees her boss looking at the clock as she slips by him on her way to her office. Once inside, Kim plops herself into her chair and is about to lay her head on her desk, when her secretary enters to remind her of the two appointments she has this morning. *"Oh..., can you please reschedule those for me, I simply uh.., have too much to do today,"* Kim replies, as she shuffles some paper and points to her computer.

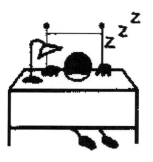

Alone in her office, Kim closes her eyes and nods off.

Sometimes we'd like put things off simply because we are too exhausted. In that case giving in may well be the right thing to do.

Unfortunately we are not always able to take such liberties, for instance, when we are on company time.

Since tiredness can be a very overwhelming sensation, but *"sorry boss, I'm a bit fatigued, so I'll be slacking off today,"* usually does not go over too well, we are inclined to think up excuses in order comply with the innate desire to rest or take it easy.

Rings a bell? If so

√   **Admit** you are bagged and **give in** if you can. You will probably do a better, and in certain cases a safer job, when you are bright-eyed and bushy-tailed.

√   If you are unable to give in to your desire to rest, **do**:
- take a 15 minute walk or jog, preferably in the morning when the air is still cool.
- work in a well-ventilated, preferably sun-lit space. Poor air can make you even more sleepy, while dim lighting can deregulate your body's natural clock.
- have some coffee, but not too much.
- drink lots of water.
- laugh!
- stay away from tedious chores and boring people.

don't:
- overeat, skip meals, or feast on sugary snacks. After the initial boost, you'll come crashing down.
- drink alcohol.

√   For future reference, and if at all possible, never again let anything come in between you and your **eight hours** of sleep.

√   Certain **medications** can cause fatigue. If you are taking any, check for its side-effects.

√   If you have trouble sleeping, find out what the cause may be (e.g. noise, worry, bumpy mattrass), and deal with it.

√   If you seem to get enough sleep, but you are still tired all the time, go see your doctor. Prolonged mental or physical weariness may be a **sign** of more serious physiological, emotional or mental problems, and should not be ignored.

Reason 10: Stress

Today's To do List:

- ☐ smooch with spouse
- ☐ walk the dog
- ☐ wake, dress, feed, and drop off kids
- ☐ call the plumber
- ☐ pay bills
- ☐ return phone calls
- ☐ reschedule business meeting
- ☐ doctor's appointment at 10 am
- ☐ finish the proposal
- ☐ drop off keys
- ☐ clean out closet
- ☐ parent \-teacher meeting at 2:15 pm
- ☐ ....

Most of us can easily handle the physical aspects that come with the hustle and bustle of daily life. It is our mind, however, that is doing hard time while it tries to arrange, schedule, keep up and remind us of the chores we need to tackle. As the heat goes up for our mind, so does our stress level. Stress is usually **pressure** on the **mind**, something we can only take so much of before it becomes hazardous. While a little pressure can make us more productive, too much stress will do the opposite, causing us lose focus and possibly even burn out.

When we have a lot on our mind our body is triggered to release stress hormones into our system. As long as we feel we are in control of the situation at hand, our stress hormone levels will stay in check, while the rush they produce helps us focus and gives us the extra energy we need to keep up.
If, however, pressures continue to increase, and we start losing control over the state of affairs, the production of stress hormones will go into overdrive, and instead of helping us, they now start to work against us. Overwhelmed, we lose our concentration and eventually we'll come to a point that we (want to) give up.

Stress is really about control. No matter the cause(s) of tension, be it getting married, applying for a mortgage, dealing with a two-year old, suffering from PMS, anger, illness, shyness, a broken heart, or meeting a deadline, if we feel we are in control of the situation, stress is manageable.

We all like to portray a picture of being coolheaded and in control, since lack of control is often considered to be a sign of weakness and emotional instability, especially in more formal settings such as the work place. And so, rather than admitting to the fact that we have more on our plate than we can comfortably handle, we resort to excuses in an effort to lighten our load or to get away with things.

The ability to deal with tension differs from time to time: frustration and stress tend to set in sooner when we are, for instance, hungry, hot, cold, feeling under the weather, or in pain.

Proficiency to keep cool also differs from person to person: some personalities, particularly the worrier, the pessimist, the perfectionist and the control freak, are especially prone to stress since their mind is already racing with thoughts and concerns long before they are exposed to potential stressful situations.

Chronic mental tension can lead to irritability, hostility, anger, resentment, anxiety, tics, phobias, obsessions, depression, mental fatigue and burnout, but it can also play itself out on the body.

Stress can weaken our immune system, making us more prone to viral, bacterial, and fungal infections.
It also increases our risk of cancer, heart disease, stroke, ulcers, stomach problems, and obesity, as well as muscular tension, head, neck and backaches, and can contribute to sleep disturbances and sexual dysfunction.

Rings a bell? If so

√   **Admit** that stress may have gotten the best of you.

√   Here are some ways to manage stress:

   ◆ **Reduce your stress:**
Make a list of all your stressors, then deal and do away with them the best you can. If you are stressed out because someone angers you, try and talk things out with this person.

   ◆ **Accept you limitations**:
You too, oh mighty perfectionist, controller, high achiever and adrenaline junkie, are merely human. Set attainable goals and only take on what you can manage.

   ◆ Learn to say: **"Sorry, but no can do."**

   ◆ **Change your mind:**
Excessive worry and pessimism can bring us to a screeching halt even before we run into actual stressful situations. Changing our views, expectations and thought processes is very difficult, but can be done through awareness and determination.

   ◆ **Be flexible:**
Rigid thinking only ads to the level of stress as it obstructs our ability to search for solutions, to problem solve, and to be creative.
Open-mindedness also helps look at the whole picture and put things in perspective: what is stressing you out right now, will probably not matter too much when you look back at it, at the age of eightyfive.

♦ **Be a team player:**
If your favourite saying is *"If you want things done right, you need to do it yourself,"* you are, besides being controlling, setting yourself up for additional work and undue stress.
Put some trust in the abilities of your fellow man and start sharing the work. (Okay, if it makes you feel better, you may handpick the people you work with).
Sometimes it also helps to let go of the notion that your way is the only right way. Be open to other people's input, who knows, you might learn something.

♦ Learn to say: **"Can you give me a hand, please?"**

♦ **Get a load off:**
Stress can be very draining and to get re-energized and maintain our ability to cope, we need to once in a while get our mind off things. We can accomplish this by doing something we find distracting and enjoyable, such as doing crossword puzzles, spending time on a hobby, volunteering, or even watching TV.
We can also rest our mind by practising relaxation techniques such as meditation, breathing exercises, Yoga, or Tai Chi.

♦ **Eat sensibly:**
Too much food can make us lethargic. Lack of nutrients and vitamins leaves us feeling depleted. Both lower our ability to cope.

♦ **Get physical:**
A walk in the park, a swim, or a good work-out at the gym can reduce stress levels, as well as help us cope better with pressure.

- **Sleep well:**
  It's a new stressful day! Feeling refreshed from a good night's sleep will help you get through it.

- **Laugh a little:**
  A sense of humour about matters can release tension.

- **Have a good support system in place:**
  Having good friendships, family, neighbourhood, club member, and other social and spiritual relationships in place, not only gives us more chances to get out and play and get re-energized, but also more opportunity to share our feelings and concerns. Talking to someone we trust can be very helpful in alleviating stress.

Last, but not least:

- **Practice simplicity:**
  In order to keep our sanity in this fast and furious world, we sometimes have to let go of certain things and remember that what we want is not always what we need.

And then there is the stress-related procrastinator of a different kind: **the adrenaline junkie:**
When we are under pressure our body produces adrenaline, a chemical that can be as exciting and addictive as any other drug out there. As such, some of us will - often subconsciously - yet purposely, leave things to the last minute to build pressure and so induce the rush that comes with the influx of adrenaline. Apparently certain individuals find fried nerve endings is a small price to pay for getting things done.

To each their own, I guess...

Reason 11: Boredom

Jared's Story:

Jared lives in a house,
that is indeed quite quaint.
His white picket fence, however,
is in dire need of some paint.

So go Jared, go
to the Home Depot.
And set your sight,
on a lovely white.

With brush in hand,
Jared paints, but... on no!
He still had over one,
hundred pickets to go!

Jared stops and thinks:
"This job is so dull, it stinks!
So, instead I'll just go,
Have a brew with my bro!"

Sometimes a chore fails to grab, or maintain, our interest and so we may be easily swayed to shelve or abandon the task because we find it boring.

Although we all should be able to see ourselves through the occasional drab job, we should definitely take note if feeling bored seems to become the norm rather than the exception in our life.

We have been wired to be active and creative, to explore and play, to manipulate and to seek social interaction, not only to learn and broaden our horizons, but also because it makes life more interesting and diverse, thus more worthwhile hanging on to.

If we, for some reason or another, can't get excited about anything over a prolonged amount of time, we will eventually lose the capacity to actively focus our attention and interact altogether. Over time, this can cause us to withdraw even from environments and activities we once found alluring, but also render us helpless in coping and changing our situations.

Animals in captivity often suffer from chronic boredom, causing them to take on all types of unusual and often self-destructive behaviours, such as continuous rocking, pacing, pulling hair or feathers, and gnawing at their own limbs.

We too tend to take on abnormal, frequently self-directed, and self-defeating behaviours, such as overeating, overspending, abusing alcohol and drugs, or doing other things "for kicks" in an ill attempt to ease the suffering that comes with boredom.

Rings a bell? If so:

√ **Admit it:**
The project bores you.

√ **Accept it:**
It's a fact of life. Some things just need to get done, fun or no fun.

√ **Work with it:**
Focus on the **gain**, rather than the pain.
Few things in life come without a price. Imagine how beautiful your picket fence will look with a fresh coat of paint, rather than concentrating on how boring the chore itself will be.

√ **Play it:**
We are in a waiting room when we pick up a magazine and read an interesting article, we watch the soaps while running the treadmill, we listen to music while washing the walls... and it dawns on us that the waiting doesn't seem so long and our routines and chores don't seem so boring. This is because we managed to find a **stimulus elsewhere** and, allowing the dull task to ride on its coat tails, it becomes bearable after all. It is a bit of a mind trick, but it works. So next time the weeds need pulling, for your added pleasure, do it when your yummy neighbour happens to be outside too!

√ **Chip it:**
Spread monotonous and time-consuming chores over smaller and more tolerable **increments**. Three days of two-hour boredom may be easier to handle than one solid day of utter drab and internal suffering.

√ **Move it:**
For some of us the hardest part is to start or pick things up where we left off. Commit yourself to get going anyway, even if it is with the intention of just doing it for a short while. Once we have set things in motion the power of momentum often will do the rest.

√ **Reward it:**
While the sense of completion can be quite rewarding in itself, there is nothing wrong with making things even more gratifying. Yes, I think you've earned that manicure after toiling in the yard all weekend.

√ **Pass it:**
If all else fails, pull out your wallet and **pay** someone to tackle the job.

√ **Watch it:**

Be happy often, and we will dispose our mind, and so ourselves, to be that way in general.

Be angry or annoyed on a regular basis and our mind programs itself as that being the preferred way to be.

Be bored for a prolonged amount of time, and at a certain point our brain will know of no other way.

Given that our mind tends to take a stance of *"if you can't beat em, join em"*, it is important to keep at least our negative emotions in check, and take care that they do not get the upper hand in the long run.

√ **Cure it:**

Nature wired us to feel a sense of boredom not to pester us, but for the purpose of warning us that something is amiss. It urges us to seek change or stimulus before we go "out of our mind".

Chronic Boredom is often a precursor of depression, a state of mind you don't want to be in. If you feel persistently weary, it may be time to seek outside help.

Reason 12: Impatience

Meet Robin:

Robin is in need of new checks and so today she joins the end of the line-up at her bank. She waits, and waits, and waits some more. Things are not moving too swiftly and soon she finds herself getting restless. Unpleasant thoughts begin to cross her mind as she looks at some of the people in front of her: *"Why doesn't she pay her bills at the bank machine?" "And look at that guy, next time roll your coins at home man, you're holding up the friggin' line!"* Robin glances at her watch once more. *"Oh, to hell with this, I'll get the checks some other time!* She steps out of line and storms out the building.

Gone are the days of endless crochet or wood carving...
In our world of planes, trains, and automobiles, quicky weddings, ready-in-three-minutes dinners, and highspeed internet, we are no longer taught the virtue of patience and fortitude. The irony is that despite, or should I say because, of our ever-increasing intolerance for delay and "wastage" of time, it is our very need for instant gratification that often causes us to procrastinate or cop out, and as such... cause delay and wasted time. Robin didn't want to hang about, so she walks away only to have to go back to the bank and stand in line *again* at a later date. We don't want to spend the time upgrading ourselves, yet we willing to

waste precious years filling a mind-numbing job. We stay in a bad relationship, because we can't stomach the prospect of having to "go through the whole spiel again" with someone new. In our pursuit of immediate relief we often sell ourselves short by not doing the things we should be doing to be better off in the long run.

Rings a Bell? If so:

√ **Admit** you are impatient.

√ Remember that patience is a virtue. If not for that, learn it to remain **healthy**. Impatience has lead to many an elevated blood pressure, anxiety attack, heart attack and stroke.

√ Next time your patience is tested, take a **long deep breath,** hold it for a few seconds, then slowly exhale. Repeat if necessary. It will help you cope.

√ Focus on the **result** you want, rather than the **time** it takes.

√ Practice **patience-building** tasks.
Go fishing, do a puzzle, pick up knitting. You may also find that these time-consuming actions actually help you relax.

√ **Think** of the last time your impatience truly did you any good. I'm waiting...

√ **Lighten up!** Sometimes we are so focused on being responsible, functional, practical, efficient and productive, that we end up procrastinating about being playful.
Inability to use time "frivolously" can keep us from doing fun things, and from pursuing dreams that seemingly serve no purpose other than giving us some enjoyment.

Reason 13: The Blues

Meet Helen:

Helen is alone on her couch, her eyes red and swollen.
She feels tired and drained, and she hasn't eaten anything
of sustenance in days.
She feels cold, her head hurts
and her stomach is upset.
But all this does not compare to
the dull yet all-consuming ache
she feels in the depths of her
chest.

Seeking comfort under her
blanket, her face is wet with
tears. Unable to control her
sobbing, Helen rolls herself into
a tight fetal position,   as if to
desperately hold on and protect
her breaking heart.

Feelings of loss, sorrow, despair, loneliness, emptiness,
hopelessness, worthlessness: we will all at times face events or
circumstances in life that will cause us to feel sad and down.

It is natural to feel joyless after a particular loss or trauma.
Withdrawal is part of the healing process as it allow us to "lick
our wounds", collect our thoughts, and seek closure.
During that period we often don't feel like doing much else,
 but with time we usually manage to get over and on with things,
so we will once more be able to focus on our responsibilities
and attend to our needs and wants.

Sometimes however, the blues won't pass, or seem to recur on a regular basis. This can have several causes:
- ♦ we get stuck somewhere in the process of grieving over a notable event,
- ♦ we feel a sense of inadequacy or helplessness, or general lack of control over our life,
- ♦ we suffer from a biochemical imbalance.

While procrastination can have a negative impact on our well-being, feeling down causes us to further linger and procrastinate, making us feel even more miserable.

Rings a bell? If so:

√ **Admit** you're down or depressed.

√ Try to **identify** what is causing you to feel this way.

√ If your sadness is due to a **specific event**, such as break-up or job loss, allow yourself time to grief.
Be kind to yourself and surround yourself with people who care, while gradually gearing yourself to picking up the pieces and getting on with your life.

√ If you feel you are getting stuck in the grieving process, or sense that your depressed mood may have another cause, it may be time to seek outside help.

Reason 14: Guilt or Shame

Meet Ann:

Ann has been married to Kevin for the last twelve years and they have two pre-teen children together. Their relationship has been loveless for a long time.

Due to Kevin's violent outbursts toward Ann, she and the children have had to seek refuge at the local women's shelter on more than one occasion. While Kevin has been repeatedly abusive toward Ann, he has never physically hurt the children who, by the way, seem to adore him.

At times Kevin feels bad and promises to seek help, but has yet to live up to his word.

Lately Ann has been suspecting Kevin of having an affair with a woman at work, but in all honesty Ann doesn't care since she feels nothing for Kevin anymore.

Meanwhile, Ann often feels empty and lonely. Sometimes she plays with the idea of taking the kids and leaving

Kevin, only to be overcome by guilt because she would be *"ripping the kids away from their father,"* and shame for *"having failed at her marriage".*

And so she stays, telling herself, her family, and her friends it's not so bad.

A healthy sense of guilt and shame allows us to be accepted, and find belonging and protection within society, thus improving our chances for survival.

Nature wired most of us with the ability to develop a sense of conscience; it is our social environment, however, that teaches us - mainly during our childhood - *when* to feel guilt and shame, and to *what extent* we should be feeling these, by bestowing us with their going morals, limits and expectations.

As we internalize our surroundings' standards and beliefs, we slowly replace our caregiver's limit setting by our own Inner Critic (that voice inside us with whom we have an inner dialogue going when we are faced with sensitive issues). This is where guilt and shame find their tremendous power: with the Inner Critic in place, guilt and shame become **self-burdening emotions**. Punishments we, in a way, put upon ourselves when we violate, or threaten to violate, the going moral standards. As such we no longer need anyone else to give us an emotional licking; we can now do that all by our lonesome.

Since we can't walk away from our Inner Critic this can be an especially hounding and unpleasant experience.

Guilt and shame differ from each other in that we can feel guilt whether or not we ever get "found out', whereas shame tends to only take form when our actions become, or threaten to become publicly known.

Either way, when we are faced with having to make decisions that are unfavourable or, we feel, go against a moral code, guilt and shame can cause us to procrastinate.

Rings a bell? If so:

√   **Admit** you are struggling with feelings of guilt and/or shame.

√   If you sense guilt or shame is what is holding you back, the first thing you need to do is to separate **rational** from **irrational** feelings, so you will be able to determine if your delay is for good reason, or is in fact needless.

Individuals suffering from irrational guilt or shame often have two sets of rules: one overly strict one for themselves (instilled during childhood and generally based on old fashioned values), and one more relaxed for the rest of the world (and usually based on more current values).

An effective way to determine if your sense of guilt or shame is excessive or ungrounded, is to imagine someone else, preferably someone you like, in your predicament.
This will cause you to switch to your more relaxed set of rules and enables you to draw a more objective conclusion:

Ann imagined her pre-teen daughter to be older and in an abusive and loveless relationship, and came to the conclusion she would not only understand and approve, but even *encourage* her daughter to get out. It became clear to Ann that she had been too hard on herself.

√   If you feel you have good grounds to feel guilt or shame, then you may not be procrastinating at all, but rather trying to stop yourself from doing something you shouldn't be doing in the first place.

√ And then there are those situations where you feel you are "damned if you do and damned if you don't."
When faced with a **moral dilemma**, it is sometimes best to not get too hung up on what discomfort your perspective choices may initially cause, but rather focus on what result they may bring about in the long run.

√ Make a decision!

√ Try to do the right thing.

√ Learn to swallow your pride. It gets us in trouble far too often!

and finally

√ Learn to forgive yourself. Sometimes we can do little more than admit we f-**beep**-d up.
Learn from your mistakes. Pay your dues the best you can, and get on with it.

Reason 15: Out of habit

Their mission: to infiltrate and dominate every aspect of our life and our very being. Lurking from the dark, they patiently wait for the right time to enter our life and gradually and unknowingly take over our bodies, penetrate our minds, and take control of our behaviours and actions. While most of them are good-natured (in fact, we would hardly be able to live with out them), some of them clearly seek to harm, even destroy. All need not be lost however, for with courage and determination we have the power to beat the Bad while finding an ally in the Good.

- Habitus Persistus -

The above reads a bit like a Sci-fi thriller (okay, a B-rated one), but it really isn't all that exciting: "They" are merely our **habits**. Be it smoking, positive thinking, throwing temper tantrums, or practising good oral hygiene, habits are learned motor, physical, perceptual, cognitive and affective patterns of activity that, through repetition, become dominant, effortless and routine.

Challenge: what is and is not, is in the eye of the beholder, and defined by the actions and behaviours we take on in our quest to deal with it. Research, further investigation, taking action, withdrawal or avoidance are some practices we may engage in as a result of us facing a challenge; practices which can quickly become habitual ways of coping.
Procrastinate often enough in the face of challenge and this behaviour too can turn into a habit, and once in place it becomes hard to give up.

Rings a bell? If so:

√   **Admit** you may be a habitual procrastinator.

√   Habits find their power in that they happen without us usually giving them a second thought. By becoming **consciously aware** of the behaviour we can fight it at will, if necessary.

√   Most habits serve more than one **purpose**.
Take smoking for instance: besides it being addictive, smoking may allow us to fit in with our peers, help us deal with stress or anxiety, give us oral gratification or simply something to do.
The more reasons we have for engaging in a habit, the harder it generally is to break, since every one reason represents one more potential hurdle we need to overcome..
Knowledge is power, though, and knowing exactly what makes a habit appealing to us, can greatly help us in breaking a bad routine.
So, what is the purpose behind you routinely procrastinating?

√   The most successful way of breaking a bad habit, including the one of procrastination, is not just by erasing it, but by **replacing** it with a **good routine**. You may, for instance, rather than avoidance, commit yourself to focus on the perks that come from completing the task, get into the habit of writing down possible solutions or goals, or take a deep breath and face things head-on.

√   The ticket to change is **consistency**. We fell into a bad habit by doing the same wrong thing over and over again.
By committing ourselves to persistently behave well in the face of challenge we will eventually create a good habit.

Part IV

Getting rid of
the
Ball and Chain:

✓ The Path to Needless Delay
   (and how we have Choices every Step of the Way)
✓ The making of a Change

• 1 •

The Path to Needless Delay

In our quest to stop procrastinating it is important that we come to understand how we get from feeling a need, to eventually behaving a certain way, because while this process is fairly straightforward, each step can hold the cause and so the solution, to our lingering.

Let's clarify this process by identifying its components with the help of a flow chart and an example. Possible sacrifices are indicated by: **($)**

A leaking faucet at Betty and Bob's place.

I   Bob has noticed that the faucet in the kitchen has been leaking for a few days now, and it is starting to annoy him. Bob feels the **need** to fix the faucet.

Betty, Bob's wife, had become aware of the dripping too, and is happy Bob is willing to take on the task.

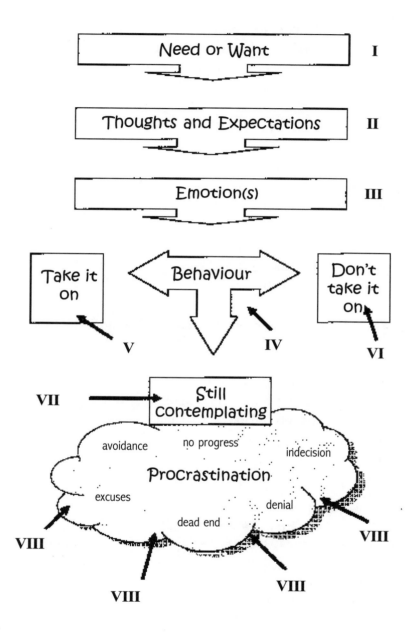

II As Bob takes another look at the faucet, his mind is flooded by **thoughts** and **expectations**.
"I have to figure out what is wrong." **($)**
"It's the washer, I can get one at the hardware store." **($)**
"I'm a handy guy, I can do this." **($)**
or maybe:
"Knowing me, I'll probably make things worse." **($)**

III On the way to the hardware store Bob's most predominant thoughts and expectations cause his body to produce certain chemicals, which allow Bob to feel certain emotions.

IV What Bob feels will heavily influence (but not necessarily determine) his **behaviour** and **course of action**.
Here are some possible scenario's:

V Let's say Bob feels hopeful and confident:
"Not a problem!"
"I'm a master, sometimes I just amaze myself!"
Bob has a positive outlook on the situation. He is not wondering or worried about the chore. There is little sacrifice to be made and so the risk of Bob procrastinating is low. He will likely **take on** and **complete** the task shortly.

VI Maybe Bob feels overwhelmed **($)**:
"No way am I doing this!" **($)**
"I'm phoning Pete the Plumber." **($)**
The chore worries Bob, yet he is willing to admit he feels in over his head. So Bob makes a U-turn and goes home to phone Pete. **($)**
While Bob chose **not to take on** the task, he is not procrastinating, because he is not making any excuses about it **($)**, and in fact settles the matter by phoning Pete the Plumber.

VII Maybe Bob feels a bit confused **($)**:
"I'll have to read my handyman book first." **($)**
"Maybe to store has a how-to pamphlet." **($)**
Bob is still contemplating, as he has to acquire some more knowledge **($)** before he can determine his line of action. If Bob is willing to make the sacrifice of doing some research, then Bob will probably end up completing the task. If Bob is not willing to exert himself learning, yet is not prepared to admit to this, chances are he will come up with an excuse to avoid the task of fixing the faucet.

VIII Maybe Bob feels overwhelmed **($)** and ashamed **($)**:
"What if I flood the house?" **($)**
"Stupid me, I don't know how to change a simple washer!" **($)**
"If Betty finds out, she's going to laugh at me!" **($)**
Bob has a lot to wonder and worry about and fears he can't do the task. This time it is embarrassment that gets the better of Bob. Shame - justified or not - is a particularly hard feeling to deal with **($)**, let alone admit to **($)**, and so Bob may opt to avoid his dilemma by making no move at all, while covering up the delay he causes with excuses.
"The hardware store closed early."
"They ran out of washers."
And so the act of procrastination takes form. While drips continue to drop and Betty's patience is running out, Bob is regularly reminded of his incompetence and shame. Trying to ease his suffering, he will continue to make excuses, until he either comes clean **($)**, or Betty is fed up and takes care of the leaky faucet herself.

As you may have noticed, each step of the process can carry numerous sacrifices, all of which have the potential to impede the pursuit of our need or want. Fortunately, we can also manipulate every step to change how we look upon these sacrifices. When we catch ourselves procrastinating it is important to back up and find out where the problem(s) lie, so we can deal and do away with them.

I Occasionally the problem lies with the actual need or want. It could be **unrealistic** or **infeasible**, and unable to see or admit this, we set ourselves up for failure from the get go.

Sometimes we have to come to accept that our need or want as such is unattainable, and that we have to adjust it, leave it to someone better equipped, or sometimes even completely let go of it. Having to do the latter can be particularly difficult and painful if it involves a lifelong dream.

II Thoughts and expectations can get us into trouble too, and are heavily influenced by:

Personal Experience:
The knowledge gained from living, or hearing about, certain occurrences in the past, can leave us with a biased view on similar events we face in the present or future.

An individual with, for instance, mostly positive experiences regarding job search, will probably feel more hopeful about finding gainful employment in the future, than someone with mainly negative experiences under his belt.

(Pre)disposition and behaviour patterns:
Our psychological make-up further affects our perceptions. An introvert, for example, will have a different view on making friends than an extrovert.

A student with a propensity for worry will, despite her possible good experiences in the past, still see midterm exams in a different light than a peer with a more optimistic or laid-back disposition.

The social systems we are part of:
What is important to us, and what values and morals we live by, can greatly differ from one social setting or society to the next.

Becoming aware of our previous experiences, our strengths and weaknesses, and our understanding of the social norms, and how they may affect and possibly contort our perceptions, can help us change how we look upon challenge and sacrifice.

III When it comes to our emotions keeping us from taking action, we have to be watchful for two things:
Mixed emotions:
We have bills to pay and so we may initially feel positive about our need to be employed. The secondary gains or advantages that come with not working, however (e.g. more free time, ability to sleep in), can ultimately leave us with contradicting feelings about holding a job. Should we decide to remain unemployed, we will likely try to cover up our reasons for inaction with excuses rather than expose our true motives, since these are generally considered less than noble in the eyes of others.
Distorted emotions:
Emotional wounds can leave us with distorted emotions, such as irrational guilt, shame or doubt, displaced anger, or excessive worry. Warped emotions can be especially powerful and can easily sway us to come to unwise decisions or engage in damaging behaviours.

IV Most **behaviour patterns** are developed during childhood by following example set by our primary caregivers and the social systems we are part of. They are adapted throughout life by further observation and life experiences.
If we can't seem to find the reasons for our lingering in any of the previous steps, then it may be time to take a closer look at what we taught to do in the face of chores or challenge. Who knows, maybe we come from a line of couch potatoes, or maybe

we were taught to rely on others to take care of our needs or wants. Behaviour patterns are hard to break once they are in place, but it can be done if we are willing to set our mind to it.

V Sometimes we have no problems commencing action, yet run into trouble when it come to **seeing the task through**. Staying focused can be difficult at times:

- ◆ **Lack of planning** can cause us to lose track of what needs to be done in order to meet our need or want.
- ◆ Unexpected **complications** can discourage us from completing a task.
- ◆ **Temptation** to do something else can be hard to resist, especially when the task at hand is boring, unappealing, or overwhelming.
- ◆ Our **impatience** can cause us to abandon a task that is taking "too long".

How we deal with these potential stumbling blocs depends on our willingness to do **research** and **set goals**, on our ability to **detect** and **solve problems**, and our **determination** to meet our need or want; factors we can all manipulate at will.

VI Choosing to not (personally) pursue our need or want is perfectly fine, as long as it is somewhat morally correct, we are open and honest about it, and we are truly at peace with our resolution.

Giving up a dream can hurt. Resentment after the fact could be a sign that we have not yet come to terms with the reality of our decision. Bitterness may also indicate that the need or want we had, is too important to us to ignore after all.

VII Although both **contemplation** and procrastination cause delay, the behaviours differ from each other in that we contemplate to help ourselves come to an informed and hopefully sensible decision, whereas we procrastinate to avoid having to

make any type of decision, or take further steps, at all.
Since the line between the two behaviours is so fine, it can lead us to believe we are spending time contemplating, when we are really wasting it procrastinating.

It takes **awareness** and possibly some prodding, but always a dose of **maturity** to admit to the fact that deep down inside we know exactly if, when, and why are procrastinating.
What's more, we can change our ways by **changing our minds**, and by and **doing**.

You'll be glad you did.

• 2 •

The Profile of
a Doer

W hether it is to right a wrong, to simplify, or to make your life more enjoyable, if you are ready to meet some needs and wants and make some changes, read on and learn what distinguishes a Doer from a Mean-toer:

The Doer has a continued **curiosity** for life and himself.

He delves into an awareness that allows him to recognize what he wants and doesn't want out of life.

The Doer knows what roles he wants to play, and what values he wants to live them by.

He understands he needs to challenge and review his roles and values once in a while, since he knows they can change over time. The Doer is aware of his strengths as well as his weaknesses.

The Doer **does**.

Rather than taking a stance of "just being", and possibly being miserable, she prefers to take action.

If the need arises she saves herself, instead of waiting to be saved.

The Doer trusts his **Common sense** and **Insight**.

He doesn't wait for "signs", "messages", or "(divine) intervention". He doesn't have to, because his Inner Voice gives him direction.

The Doer aims for **Growth** and **Balance**.

She strives to thrive in every aspect of her life.

She is driven by her values and strengths, rather than her wounds and weaknesses. In doing so the Doer protects herself from getting re-injured, and so promotes her personal growth and emotional healing. This allows the Doer to further find balance and contentment in life.

The Doer tries to double up when it comes to **motivation**. Whereas both the Mean-toer and the Doer may be driven by the end result of meeting a need or want, the Doer often manages to get a rush out of the pursuit itself.

The doer has **perseverance**.

While she may dislike delays, obstacles or failure just as much as the next person, it doesn't discourage her. On the contrary, for the true Dogged Doer it just got interesting.

The Doer **believes** he can.

He has confidence in himself and his abilities.

The Doer's can-do mentality and general optimism keep him focused.

What the Doer lacks in confidence she makes up in **Courage**. She doesn't shy away from, once in a while, just taking a calculated leap and freefalling for a bit, until she finds her footing again.

The Doer is willing to **take Risks** and **make Sacrifices**.

Like everybody else, he too has blocs such as doubt, fatigue, lack of knowledge, or secondary gains, which can keep him from pursuing his needs or wants. The Doer has faced these barriers head on, and has come out on top.

The Doer is **Solution focused**.

Problems arising before or during the pursuit of a need or want are dealt with accordingly.
The Doer is willing to "go back to the drawing board", get informed or do further research.
She is flexible and creative, and is able to ask for help or assistance, should the need arise.

The Doer is not afraid to make **mistakes**.

He understands that trial and error is part of the process. Rather than getting discouraged by his slip ups, the Doer learns from them, and then gets on with it.

The Doer has an ability to **visualize the end result** in such a way that for her it almost becomes real before its time, allowing the Doer to have a mental taste of what is to come. This is another powerful motivator.

The Doer has an **Action Plan**.
He can picture the road ahead, and has figured out what steps he needs to take in order to meet his need or want. To avoid becoming overwhelmed and possibly discouraged, the Doer makes sure he is informed, comes prepared, and is well organized.

The Doer sets attainable **Goals** and **Sub-goals**.
She knows that each goal she meets, will give her a sense of accomplishment, which boost her confidence to tackle the next.
Setting sub-goals protects the Doer from getting discouraged, overwhelmed, or bogged down, since she now has more than one way to meet her main goal.
Should a certain sub-goal give her particular trouble, she has the option to focus on another one, and continue to move forward until she is ready to take on the more demanding task.

The Doer practices **discipline**.
The Doer is prepared make sacrifices and is restrained by his personal values and morals.
He is able to delay gratification and resist temptation. This said, the Doer also understands the importance of taking time out to relax and re-energize, in order to avoid imbalance or burnout.

The Doer is open to **input**.
She is accepting of the fact that her way may not always the best way, nor the only way, and so the Doer welcomes other people's suggestions and opinions.

She is willing to take in constructive criticism, but chooses to shrug of the destructive kind.

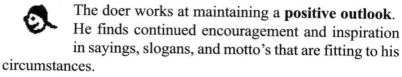 The doer works at maintaining a **positive outlook**. He finds continued encouragement and inspiration in sayings, slogans, and motto's that are fitting to his circumstances.

The Doer also insists on surrounding himself with people who are accepting of his need or want, and supportive of him pursuing it.

Finally, Doers don't linger...

they get going!

Author's Note

I hope you enjoyed this book, and encountered a few "ah-ha!" moments while reading it.

For more information, questions, feedback, or to order additional copies, do not hesitate to visit us on the Internet at:

www.lifeworkspublishing.com

or

contact your local book store